Landon L. 6th grade - Mountain Shadows Elementary, Glendale, AZ

To my wonderful son, Landon, whose last words to me were *"Mom, keep up the bird stuff."*

Written by Balinda Fortman
Illustrated by kids. Designed by Claudia Howe.

All profits from this book are donated to:
Liberty Wildlife, Phoenix, AZ

ABOUT THE AUTHOR:

Balinda lives in Phoenix, Arizona where she works at Honeywell Aerospace and as a University Professor. She holds a Bachelor's degree in Engineering and a Ph.D. in Business Administration. During her free time, she volunteers at Liberty Wildlife Rehabilitation Organization, where she cares for raptors, rescues wildlife, and does educational programs for the public. *She is pictured here with Quanah.*

© 2014 Land On Sky Publishing
All rights reserved.
Published in the United States of America
ISBN 978-1-941865-00-2

Emma G.   8th grade - Pan American Charter School, Phoenix, AZ

It was the 4th of July and the parade was about to start. People were gathering along the streets and in the park. Soon, the parade would be coming by Liberty Wildlife.

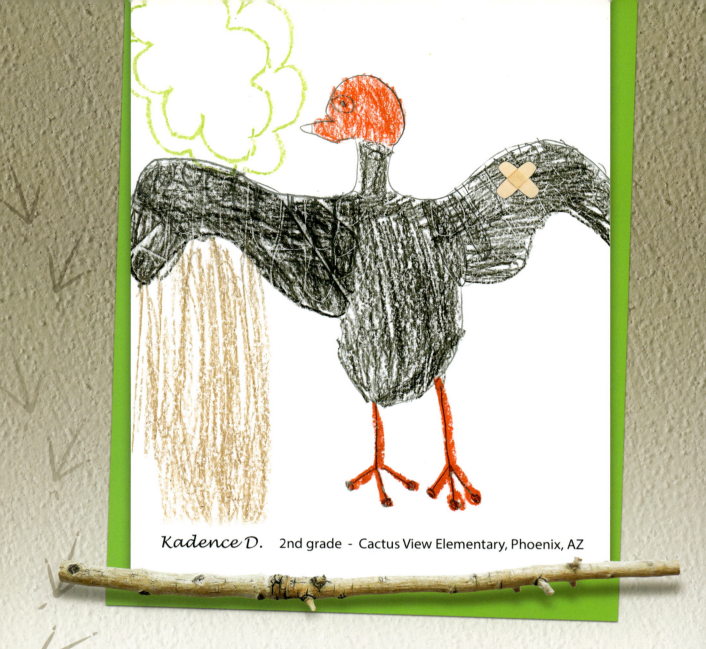

Kadence D.   2nd grade - Cactus View Elementary, Phoenix, AZ

Liberty Wildlife is a hospital for sick or injured wildlife.

Liberty Wildlife helps these animals get better so they can go back to their homes in the wild.

Andrew M. 2nd grade - Florence K-8, Florence, AZ

Some of the animals will never be able to go back to the wild because they would not survive. Even though they are better, they may not be able to hunt food to eat.

Nestor C. 8th grade - Pan American Charter School, Phoenix, AZ

But these animals can help other young animals that come to Liberty Wildlife by taking care of them and teaching them how to behave.

Roger M. 4th grade - New World Education Center, Phoenix, AZ

Sometimes these animals get to visit schools, parks, and other events so people can see them up close.

Natalie F. 2nd grade -
Cactus View Elementary, Phoenix, AZ

Quanah was coming with me to the parade that day. He came out of his cage like a perfect turkey vulture and we were waiting for the parade to come by.

"Here it comes!" I told Quanah.

Hannah P.   2nd grade - Cactus View Elementary, Phoenix, AZ

Nestor C.   8th grade - Pan American Charter School, Phoenix, AZ

There were clowns, balloons, dogs and horses. Quanah had never seen these things before.

Pretty soon, I smelled something **REALLY** bad.

Amos C.   4th grade - Casa Blanca Community School, Bapchule, AZ

Oh No!
Quanah threw up!

And it was all over my glove.

Nicholas E.   4th grade - Glenn F. Burton Elementary, Glendale, AZ

Was Quanah sick?

No, turkey vultures throw up when they are nervous or feel like they are in danger. The bad smell drives away other animals that might want to eat them or steal their food. It also makes them lighter so they can make a fast getaway.

Nielle B.   3rd grade - Casa Blanca Community School, Bapchule, AZ

Osualdo M.   3rd grade - Edison Elementary, Phoenix, AZ

I talked to Quanah softly so he would feel safe.

Soon he was relaxed and spread his wings 6 feet wide.

He was now watching the parade while soaking up the sun.

Chris P. 2nd grade - Skyline Ranch Elementary, Queen Creek, AZ

Sara B.   4th grade - Glenn F. Burton Elementary, Glendale, AZ

Turkey vultures might seem ugly at first, but they have beautiful wings that shimmer in the sun.

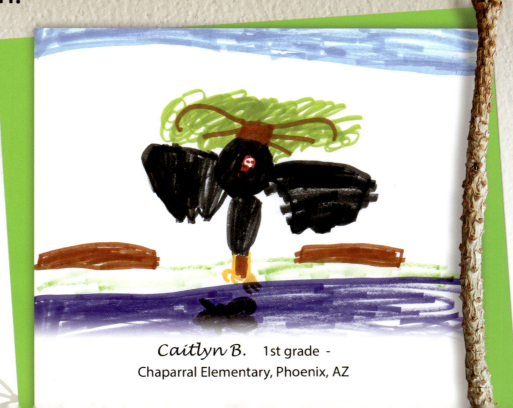

Caitlyn B.   1st grade -
Chaparral Elementary, Phoenix, AZ

They also play a very important role in nature. They help clean up some of the yucky things that could hurt us.

Kodi S.   2nd grade - Copper Basin Elementary, Queen Creek, AZ

Walter B. 8th grade - Pan American Charter School, Phoenix, AZ

Turkey vultures do not hunt and kill prey like other wildlife. They eat meat from animals that have already died.

Bill C. 3rd grade - Madison Heights Elementary, Phoenix, AZ

Sometimes, that meat can grow bacteria that would make us sick. But turkey vultures have acid in their stomach that kills bacteria and viruses.

Nolan M.   5th grade - Canyon Rim Elementary, Anaheim, CA

Everything that comes out of the back side of a turkey vulture is clean!

Perla B.   8th grade - Pan American Charter School, Phoenix, AZ

Adult turkey vultures have a bright red head with no feathers. This helps keep their head clean.

After a meal, they sit out in the sun and let the yucky stuff dry so it is easy to clean off.

Savanah H.   6th grade - Ironwood Elementary, Phoenix, AZ

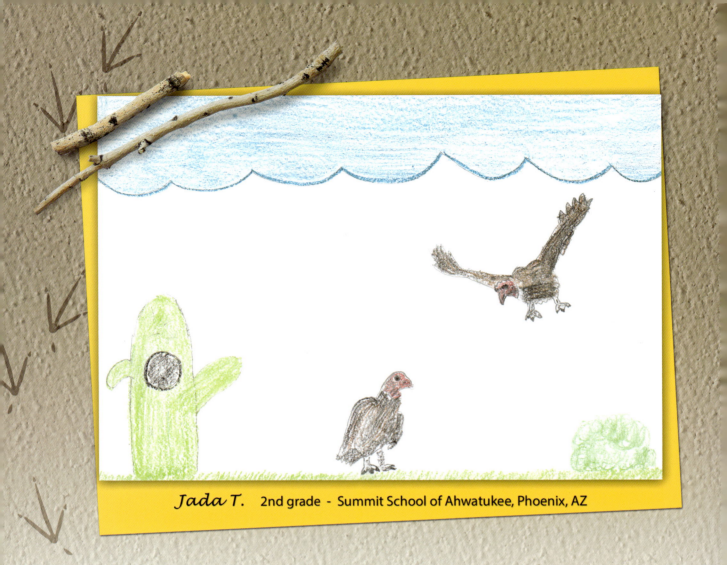

Jada T. 2nd grade - Summit School of Ahwatukee, Phoenix, AZ

To conserve energy, turkey vultures try not to flap their wings when they fly. They like to find warm pockets of air, called thermals, that rise into the sky. They hop on a thermal and ride up, up, up! From there they can glide a long way to search for food.

At night, turkey vultures can drop their body temperature several degrees while they sleep!

Katelin M.   2nd grade - Skyline Ranch Elementary, Queen Creek, AZ

Jack K.   2nd grade - Summit School of Ahwatukee, Phoenix, AZ

In the morning, they heat back up by spreading out their beautiful wings like solar panels to soak up the sun.

If a turkey vulture gets too hot, it has an unusual way to cool down. It pees on its legs! This also kills any bacteria that might be growing on its feet.

Nadine P.   8th grade - Pan American Charter School, Phoenix, AZ

Violet S.   3rd grade - Edison Elementary School, Phoenix, AZ

Turkey vultures can be found throughout the United States.

Marco C.   8th grade - Pan American Charter School, Phoenix, AZ

Adrian C. 8th grade - Pan American Charter School, Phoenix, AZ

If you see a large bird in the sky that has dark feathers on the front of its wings and grey or silver feathers in the back and is circling around in the air, then you are probably looking at a turkey vulture!

Priscilla J. 4th grade - New World Education Center, Phoenix, AZ

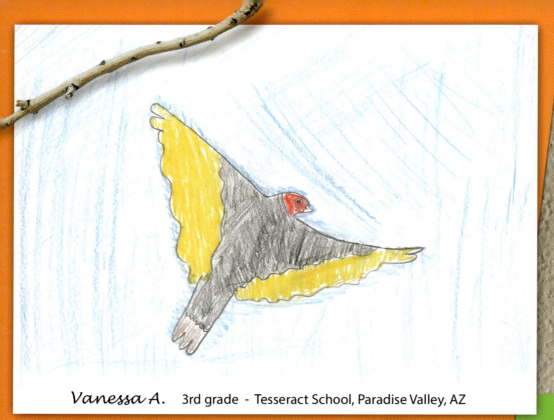

Vanessa A.   3rd grade - Tesseract School, Paradise Valley, AZ

DID YOU KNOW:

- A group of turkey vultures is called a kettle.

- Scientists once thought turkey vultures were raptors, but DNA tests indicate they belong to the stork family. (We are not going to kick them out of the raptor family, though.)

- Turkey vultures are one of the few birds of prey that have a good sense of smell and can smell food over a mile away!

Julie O.   2nd grade - Cactus View Elementary, Phoenix, AZ

HOW YOU CAN HELP

Do you like balloons? Of course! They are fun to watch, hit around, and rub on your hair to make them stick! But did you know that letting balloons go up in the sky can cause problems for birds and other animals? When animals eat balloon pieces (and they do!), they can block their digestive tract and starve.

Birds like to use the string from balloons to put in their nests. If any of the birds get tangled in the string, they may not be able to fly to get food.

HERE ARE SOME TIPS FOR HELPING WILDLIFE:

- Don't release balloons into the air.
- Keep your balloons indoors after you use them.
- When you are finished with your balloon, pop it and put it in the trash.
- Pick up balloon pieces and string you find and throw them away.

Angelina F. 4th grade - Glenn F. Burton Elementary, Glendale, AZ

Leslie Z.   8th grade - Pan American Charter School, Phoenix, AZ

QUANAH'S STORY

Quanah came to Liberty Wildlife in 2010 as a young bird with a broken right wing. The medical staff performed surgery and fixed him up the best they could, but he still gets tired when he flies. Because turkey vultures spend a lot of time flying, he would get too tired to be able to hunt for food.

Quanah now spends his days hanging with his friend Bailey (another turkey vulture) and meeting lots of people as a Liberty Wildlife Ambassador.

Quanah is now a regular at the 4th of July parade and enjoys sitting in the sun as he watches it go by.

WHAT TO DO IF YOU FIND AN INJURED BIRD:

If a baby bird has fallen out of the nest, but the parents are nearby and it does not look injured, have an adult place the baby back into the nest. It is an old wives' tale that the bird parents will not care for the baby if a human has touched it.

If you are unable to get a baby bird to a wildlife facility right away, you can soak dry puppy or kitten food in water until it is spongy. Squeeze out the excess water and offer a bit of the food to the baby on the clip end of a pen cap. This is the only food you should offer. An injured or stressed bird may not eat. Do not give water to a bird.

WHERE TO GET HELP:

For injured wildlife in Arizona, contact Liberty Wildlife at 480-998-5550.

If you are outside of Arizona, look up the number of your local wildlife rescue organizations or state wildlife agency such as Game and Fish and write them here:
_____
(that way you have them if you need them)

Ciara R. 2nd grade - Cactus View Elementary, Phoenix, AZ

WANT MORE INFORMATION?

Visit Liberty Wildlife's website at:
www.LibertyWildlife.org

Sign up for nature news at:
www.libertywildlife.org/publications/nature-news/

Check out Liberty Wildlife's blog at:
www.libertywildlife.org/publications/blog/

Join Quanah's Fan Club at:
www.landonsky.com/fanclub/quanah/

SPECIAL THANKS TO:

My wonderful "family" at Liberty Wildlife that made this possible: Megan Mosby, John Glitsos, Peggy Cole, Carol Marshall, Carol Suits, Linda Scott, Anne Payton, Terry Stevens, Kathy Haggerty, Jan and Joe Miller, Craig Fischer, Wendy Bozzi, and countless others who gave support and editing skills including (but not limited to): Michael Ziffer, Claudia Howe, Leo and Judy Fortman, Madi and Jacob Black, Shawna and Colton Patten, Jim and Jo Gass, Darrin Strosnider, Barb Del'Ve, and Cindy Gort.

Thank you to all the wonderful artists who contributed their talents.

Raptors courtesy of Liberty Wildlife.

Gage G. — 2nd grade - Cactus View Elementary, Phoenix, AZ

Turkey Vulture Gallery

Michael T.   8th grade -
Pan American Charter School, Phoenix, AZ

Arcelia S.   8th grade -
Pan American Charter School, Phoenix, AZ

Perla B.   8th grade -
Pan American Charter School, Phoenix, AZ

Michael T.   8th grade -
Pan American Charter School, Phoenix, AZ

Brian M.   8th grade -
Pan American Charter School, Phoenix, AZ

Alexander M.   2nd grade -
Skyline Ranch Elementary, Queen Creek, AZ